BRIDESTONES

Bridestones

MIRANDA PEARSON

McGill-Queen's University Press

Montreal & Kingston • London • Chicago

ISBN 978-0-2280-2077-6 (paper)
ISBN 978-0-2280-2078-3 (ePDF)
ISBN 978-0-2280-2079-0 (ePUB)

Legal deposit second quarter 2024
Bibliothèque nationale du Québec

Printed in Canada on acid-free paper that is 100% ancient forest free
(100% post-consumer recycled), processed chlorine free

Funded by the Government of Canada   Financé par le gouvernement du Canada   Conseil des arts du Canada   Canada Council for the Arts

We acknowledge the support of the Canada Council for the Arts.

Nous remercions le Conseil des arts du Canada de son soutien.

McGill-Queen's University Press in Montreal is on land which long
served as a site of meeting and exchange amongst Indigenous Peoples,
including the Haudenosaunee and Anishinabeg nations. In Kingston
it is situated on the territory of the Haudenosaunee and Anishinaabek.
We acknowledge and thank the diverse Indigenous Peoples whose
footsteps have marked these territories on which peoples of the world
now gather.

Library and Archives Canada Cataloguing in Publication

Title: Bridestones / Miranda Pearson.

Names: Pearson, Miranda, author.

Series: Hugh MacLennan poetry series.

Description: Series statement: The Hugh MacLennan poetry
series | Poems.

Identifiers: Canadiana (print) 20230580351 | Canadiana (ebook)
2023058036X | ISBN 9780228020776 (softcover) | ISBN
9780228020783 (PDF) | ISBN 9780228020790 (ePUB)

Subjects: LCGFT: Poetry.

Classification: LCC PS8581.E388 B75 2024 | DDC C811/.54—dc23

This book was typeset by Marquis Interscript in 9.5/13 Sabon.

for Dill Anstey

… and the emptiness

turns its face to us

and whispers

"I am not empty,

I am open"

From "Vermeer" by Tomas Tranströmer

CONTENTS

Contents

Contents

1/

THE WHITE ROOM

In a plain white room,
a window open to the west –
to the cool of early spring –
she was breathing the old language,
our first and our last.

She laboured, as if running up a hill
or in the last moments of love.
Death was ahead. She dashed for it.
Her breath filled the room, fast and panting.
Then it stopped, and I was alone.

Three days before she died,
I drew her as she slept,
head tilted back, white nightie
falling off her shoulders, become so thin.

Her never-small nose
was at its most stately,
all her ancestors lined up
there in her profile.

Yes, the sketch was made without consent.
But it was the quiet,
the cool light in the room
making an etching

of the tangled shrouds,
her sleeping head in its last hours,
that made me want
to draw them out.

PIANO

Our mother sits at the piano,
her unmistakeable stoop, her narrow back.
I didn't know she could play, but here,
neck exposed like Marie Antoinette,
she's picking out the notes –
Grief, of all things – Grieg –

COME

Come, anguish. Help us manage
the plainsong of an open shore,

its language of high tide rich and close,
close and hard to see.

Rinse and empty, heat-breath
of my mouth, soul-statement

of a self that's more shadow
than archaeological clue.

Walking the labyrinth of things
we will no longer do.

RED KITE

I'd like to come back as human if possible.
But if not, a bird. For the flying.

I'm grief-blinkered on a local hill and she sweeps on by
as she used to sashay into a room, ta-da!

Today she's trying out the new form,
likely surprised as anyone, didn't expect to be so large,
                                                                    so regal –

and look, can just   cruise on this wingspan,
held by tender palms of air

                    ~

At thirty-seven she broke a rib flying a kite on Welsh cliffs
but she said it was still heaven – the stiff wind, the power ...

                    ~

I long to hold her strings but she's away,
roaming wind-paths high above the farms,

the town she knows so well.

She's red – which is fitting – breast and underwing a deep
russet, a rose.
Broad and wide as a cross, as the Spitfire and Hurricane

propped on display at the aerodrome.
Those plucky birds that zipped and hovered over these fields

when she was a child, when she scanned the skies as now
she scans the earth, visible and invisible.

TO A FRIEND IN DEEP MOURNING

(from *"Etiquette"* by Emily Post)

A woman alone may never use a crest
Paper for a man
Mourning paper

The note of apology
Very intimate
Engraved   Indirect

Letters no one cares to read
Letters of gloomy apprehension
Letters of petty misfortunes

The blank

The letter of the capital "I"
The letter of chronic apology
The dangerous letter

The letter of the two wives
The letter no woman should write
Devices for stamping

The complimentary closing
The intimate closing
Other endings
Folding a letter
Sealing wax

One last remark –

CLEARANCE

The bright morning we laid the ashes
sunlight flickered and

danced over the empty walls –
windblown flame.

Now, two lie stashed in loam together,
their bones and flesh reshuffled to ash,

garlanded with foxglove,
primroses, and snowdrops

~

I stay on in the house. Sit Shiva.
Still with her, the thick smell of her hair,

her clothes, her kitchen.
Warm and distinct.

How one grief
may throw no light upon another.

I look at shadows cast by lamps,
the short queue of hollow boots.

Hold recipes in her handwriting

~

Living in her house is like
being in her body again,

tending the house and garden
is tending her.

The house is entwined with her
and I lie in its belly,

an adult foetus
in a dead mother

~

Get going girl. Strike the set.
Dismantle the scenery and gilt,

lift down paintings
by their crumbling Victorian frames –

Yorkshire Road. Seascape.
A Bowl of Cherries.

Miniature plays-within-plays,
parables nested in plain sight.

Roll the Persian rugs. Puff the dust
off books and box them up ready

for the open sea of charity

~

As the house is cleared
it reduces back to small cottage

then a shell, humble and ordinary.
This theatre of our childhood,

so powerful and charismatic to us.
Now, myth becomes transparent,

its beams and structures exposed
and the fourth wall dissolves

~

It is *her* house, it is her voice I hear.
But gradually I find

my father's stethoscope
hanging behind a mirror.

The score of "The Ride of the Valkyries"
lining a drawer.

He is appearing, at last,
his shyness, his wit –

~

A line of bottles on the windowsill,
vivid as medieval queens.

Stubborn alcoholism. Stained
red and green, subterranean.

In the winter garden
lakes of snowdrops appear overnight,

ghost-girls in their fresh white robes.
Sister dislodges them with her trowel.

And the passionflower and the
lily of the valley. We want to

carry their beauty with us when we leave,
as talismans, as sacred relics

~

Pheasants shriek and flounce,
pantomime dames, their ruffled dresses

hoiked up, croak-cry a rattled gunshot,
percussion or

explosive sneeze.

Magpies circle like undertakers,
a blooded rat is dropped

heavy on the doorstep,
a shocking gift – or warning.

And felled on the lawn, a white bird –
flag of wing upright on the green,

its open beak and stripped neck,
a mandala of feathers nearby.

Our heads are bowed

~

Sell, donate, pitch into the tip
where birds fight and wheel

above the jumbled heaps
of others' discarded visions,

once enchanted – as we were –
by materiality

~

I subtract and subtract
till I'm camping, minimally equipped.

Gaps appear as the fridge is carried off.
One by one appliances unfasten,

reveal the grey negatives
of a stove or dishwasher,

the kitchen becomes toothless.
Embarrassed.

It's like living in a dead body,
it's like living in entrails,

I tell friends, who say – not unreasonably,
"c'mon, surely it's not that bad"

~

The Covid test shows a second blue line –
echoes of pregnancies decades ago

with their various destinies.
A delivery man in a mask

drops off food, wine.
Waves from a safe distance.

I need to be witnessed, don't want to be alone,
but who would have the courage

to bring the comfort I crave?
I would eat them alive

~

Infectious anchoress, I cloister
at the start of the year

and again at the end:
A gestation of mourning

bookended by isolation and becalmed.
Put on mute.

Sorry, I think we've lost you –

~

Ghosts gust and balloon
to fill the empty rooms, their whispers

grow louder, layer and harmonize
to become sea shanties

as a storm pummels the house. Weather –
so indifferent, so morally inert –

though today it's operatic –
the willow weeps, howls, it

rends its robes. Poltergeists flip garden chairs,
they land at rakish angles.

The great ash cracks and splits,
then slings itself across the drive –

a melodramatic swoon.

~

We lose power, the house and I.
The closing nights together are calm,

marooned in candlelight, the cold
and thickening dark – an old song

turning in my head, the moon
lost behind shreds of cloud. Then,

reappearing, like love. Her face open,
                    wonderfully bright.

2/

RETURN TO THE CHATEAU

Long sleeps shredded by dream – diving again down
to the drawing room at the bottom of the lake.

Curtains open to the dripping trees, the willow,
the ash dieback. The soul has no age,

but at the birthday picnic we hear the guns,
we beat each other with sticks.

All the men I have loved are reminiscent of just one.
And now this sullen refusal to let love in, insistence

on the tired old ways. What do I care about?
Building another house of poems?

Swimming length after length
in the neighbour's green pool?

Only wallpaper keeps the wall up.
In dreams it crumbles.

While deep in the woods ivy holds up the folly.
The same old folly

even if you're on another path now,
slipping in your London shoes.

It must be the hidden father who
clipped those pictures from magazines

and collaged our childhood walls,
papering over my cursive script:

I can do accurate work
I can do accurate work

OVER THE ROCKIES

Cut gems, angles and planes, white and sparkling
like the ultrasound at the clinic where women

wear paper masks over their mouths,
distance establishes itself in another dark room.

Lying on my side on the paper bed, the gelled wand
passing again over passive breasts.

See the dark side of the slope, shadows
in their ghost life, their longing to carry on.

Love, how did we forget about each other?
Your body unfamiliar, unsafe to me now.

Yet, worse to be a brittle stranger,
the awful antiques of my family where we stand

in snobbish isolation. Have I become them,
in this refusal, this late-onset fear of the body?

Body as container of recycled grief, a carousel
of painted horses circle in the raking light.

INHERITANCE TAX

And the younger ones feasted on the old.
Inheritance, bloodless and vampiric.

Groves of silver birch grow
over sick money. Statues of English gentlefolk –

otherwise known as racists – their
tombs of hidden money, their gold caskets.

I know it hurts but it's good for you.
The stress and strain is a mark of recovery

– or sadism. Arrested men, their pale faces
boyish as they reel off the surnames of their

contemporaries from prep school,
trauma rendering their memories acute.

Sure, we rage and rebel against privilege.
But when the time is right

somehow we find a way back
to some of its better qualities.

CHILD POSE

Heavenly father (absent) and
earthly mother. The only time I felt safe

was when she, my son, and I
were all together under one roof.

Insecure attachment; she was
napping in front of the fireplace,

kicked by a passing boot.
Fear makes you smaller.

We allow the violence
because there is simply too much

to say no to. Truth that is not beauty,
but turns out to be useful.

Friday's child is loving and giving
but loyalty learned and modelled.

He was a beautiful man – only
through the intimacy of distance.

I tried to replicate him everywhere.
His spectral reach. How he teased us

with the Lear story, I didn't get it
– *how much do you love me?*

the meat, the salt. They both enjoyed
pitching us in competition,

stoking hunger when it was clear
there was not enough to go round.

EYES

When the past looks you dead
in the eye, passes you a handwritten letter

that you have to take because *you have her eyes.*
Pass on that blue-green glance,

brimful of games that a girl might play –
tennis, or cricket that summer day her eye

was struck (blood on white linen) and all
that followed, seen and unseen

disruption made cautious in the slow lane,
her sky-blue Morris Minor

with the amber indicator that did not –
her hand floating instead, queenly – left, left –

a car door that years later again flings open
and it's your blood on the floor,

on the white towel held to your face
your eyes conkers rattling on the ground.

A shivering Saturn's ring, a portal,
the doctors shadowy above you, their hands

fluttering left, left – down, now up, up –
shapes and strange lights:

circles, suns or   drifting coins,
unanchored as ghosts.

TOUCHED

The woman on Lower Sloane Street
lightly touches the cherry blossom.

It's shell-pink – her touch
is to know it, check if she's again

been fooled by Chelsea, so many
artificial flowers.

Then I saw she had a face of suffering,
like some I've seen on the wards.

Her eyes weird-glittered
in their heavy makeup, her mouth

a red cartoon. Touched?
The fragile cherry reaching –

crawling from its city basement?
The woman, in her brief gesture of hope?

Or the spy, embellishing every scene,
every innocent tableau.

JUST EAT

Tell that to the girl with stones in her pockets,
as if about to wade into a river. The one
who hid candlesticks in her bra who

sewed fishing weights into her dress hem.
The girl who donated blood to drain calories,
the girl who ate paper, who ate cat food,

who ate raw meat who ate her own vomit.
The girl who stole a sofa. The girl
who kept a power drill next to her bed,

who held a hot iron to her cheek who
plunged her hands into a hot water urn
who jumped off the Lions Gate Bridge.

The Burrard bridge, the Second Narrows.
The Golden Gate. All the girls who
sold their bodies for binge-food,

who dumpster-dived. Who lost their teeth.
The girl whose father played "Suzanne"
on repeat while he raped her, the girl

who sliced her legs, her arms, her stomach
till they were crosshatched with coral
encryption. Just eat.

GRAPEFRUIT

The youngest, unplanned one they had to take with them
long after they were done with children. Those dark B&Bs
in Devon, Yorkshire, or the Lakes. There it was in the morning,

halved in a glass bowl, its spokes and glace cherry,
its special silver spoon. Even coated with sugar it was an ordeal,
spurting and stinging and lacing your teeth with bitter pith.

I couldn't see the point but back then I ate what was served
along with the other mute guests, long-marrieds
at their grim breakfasts, gouging into upside-down breasts.

They seemed so deeply sad, as if almost dead.
That was fifty years ago, I suppose most are gone by now.
Avoid grapefruit, says the pharmacist in her white coat,

handing over the pills that have sometimes kept me alive –
white and bitter. And pills for my breasts too, taken
like St Agathas'. Grapefruit, little beachballs, so sun-like,

how could they harm me, or anyone? If thrown at close range,
maybe, or from a sixth floor balcony – no, step away –
you have a right to be here.

LEDA

Summerland peaches and apples,
the lakes and blossoms we drove through,

their bite, their juice.
Do you have it in you to do it all again?

Drive across Canada, climb mountains?
Carry those heavy canoes.

After each book, a grief.
You look up a psychotherapist,

one of his specialties is "infidelity."
Your father's laughter

as the hissing swan chased you.
Your horror as later he solidified, became

cemented into his armchair.
Here is a bag of keys I can't throw away

though who knows what locks
they would open now.

VISIT

My score is exceptionally low.
But that's only because I'm exploring my stupidity,

my fractured relationship with numbers.
What is the mass of this room, for instance?

Are you good with money? Are miles really time?
The thick, thick soup of time. Sometimes you go fast,

sometimes you go slow. After the election I thought –
not for the first time – that evil was in fact

stronger than good, love a fantasy. The pigeons
outside the hospital window insist on roosting there

despite the spikes. The spikes placed exactly
where they might want to rest.

TRAVELLERS

Crows attack the black garbage bags,
swooping down in pairs from the ash tree.

I wake from cluttered dreams of missed flights,
overflowing suitcases, long queues of refugees.

We all travel in darkness, homeless and lost,
unbolted and stupid with sorrow.

Around us soft grasses grow high, buff. Animal.
A choir of eucalyptus, its song   water over shingle.

Faces that grow more beautiful as you
study their ageing – our tattered caravans,

our little roadside fires of gaiety and hardship.

ACCIDENT

I cover my eyes at the accident on the road.
A man my son's age running along the highway,

his plaid shirt flapping, his long hair
tied back and coming loose. Cover my eyes.

There's so much I don't want to see.
Let's keep going, climb higher into the range,

where clouds journey over broken horizons,
make smoke of their layering.

This perilous landscape
empty of anything human.

CARETAKER

We are so unsettled on this earth.
My brother homeless, sleeping in a park,

at war with himself. War,
the biggest business on the planet.

Quicksand everywhere, though
now is not the time to say it,

when it's so close, lurking
in the black bear, the silent shadow,

the restlessness. Now I see
it's about letting go, not bridged,

texted, phoned, hurried back to.
Rain will make its torrents, wind

blow our power down.
But the house will not be on fire

and you will find the candles.
You will find the caretaker's number.

I am not the caretaker. I am not
the caretaker. Step forward

into the rain and wind. Loving
their cold, how they shape you.

HOTEL

The hotel is like a mother,
temporarily attentive,
warm, wealthy. Or,

the hotel is a sex worker,
a girlfriend-experience
of temporary shelter.

A long vertebrae of shadow
floats and shivers
on the flank of the Tower.

How you climbed yourself
out of there, hand over hand,
step-by-step. Word by word.

GRAVESIDE

The red-brick wall behind you is warmed by the sun,
warm as if it's alive. You lie waiting
for your friends to come back. When you died

I stopped moving for months – just sat, thinking
of all the times I kept you alive.
Your legs like alder branches, your scared eyes

seeing the world through alcohol's dirty windows.
Citizen of glass, you're looking good today –
somewhat improved by dying.

You lived surrounded by booze, its trick walls
rearranging themselves so you could never see out.
Today, listen to the air, the gulls

that wheel above us, pilots riding the air,
the cliffs of cloud. Smoke trails, sky trains.
Listen. I'm a sleepwalker too. Sightless eyes

turned to France, a misty bank twenty-one miles
over the sea's grey silk. But the drive
that drives that sea drives my red blood.

31

Window's camera, leaves fizzing,
clamouring like insects, or
children in a schoolyard.

Love: a sleepless chimera,
a mirage on the wall, unframed.

~

– but not yet – edges shift and decide,
as of yesterday, when we
flew like falcon over the Rockies

scanning their sharp-cut gems,
their glacial shove and churn,
white and brilliant –

~

Sing   *I will die of it,*
live a charming ghost life
along with all the others. Sing:
the purpose of life is to pass it·on

Sing, while you still can,
in the woods, under feathered branches,
the singing leaves.

Sing, while you still can, in the woods,
under trees curved taut like bows or
great, green, Islamic arches,

blue flowers spangled at our feet,
dripping from your mouth.

~

Larval   leaf.

Half-
hatched chrysalis.

The cocoon is a crumpled papery tent,
a lantern, full of mindless effort and

heart-breath, its impulse
to self-publish

        a spotted wing,

a clipped ticket from a husk, a
whiskery hanging leg.

Coltish Houdini,
wrestling from its crocus-cage

its crushed embrace

with itself

~

In the Italian Garden you withdraw your hand,
contagious and unknown. Slide back into shadow,
to the dark side of the slope.

~

And now field after field, flooded ragged lake
mirroring anxious rhyme of tree and cloud

and still, you reproduce yourself, you flow everywhere
your tributaries pouring past barbed wire and trench

against all who love you, kissing you for decades
sharing our open mouths our unwashed hands

in the bedrooms, the shelters, the temples, in the camps.
Millions of people sitting close together,

borders closed, then overnight – washed away.
We try and lock it down but it still seeps through.

It's in the information, the chants and songs we sing together,
it's in the bodies on the tracks.

~

While the all-seeing falcon flies alone, so high, with such vision
in her pale gold, elegant suspension.

She sees the blueish treetops, the geometry of flooded field,
loose-paned with stone.

She sees the fires in the camps, the snaking columns of people.
She sees the smokey shadows of clouds that touch the earth,

she sees her own singular shape – if earth is body and sky –
God help us – spirit.

FRUIT

The Tarot cards are on the carpet –
repeating them won't make it come out right.

How you despise the soft need
of a woman's love to fill your emptiness, your fear

of the cold plain. Safer to manoeuvre myself back
to mistress, a wisp of a person, a shadow.

I repeat myself. I'm the one afraid
you will banish me like Anna

O I challenge you with my famished mouth,
my maudlin confession.

Your eyes are diamonds in firelight. How lying there,
we fit like candied fruit in a cake, woke at dawn,

our fingers pulling at the pink sky, a foretelling
of something beautiful and always expert

at playing us against each other, feminist man
with your knack of explaining a woman's soul to her.

Or perhaps jealousy is the only emotion I thrive on,
gnawing at the marrow of it like a dog in an alley

while inside another bright house –
your mouth on her marzipan fruit.

DOOR

How I love your clean freckled hands, the careful way
they attend to things – the pouring of milk, the unlocking

and locking of a door. Undoing buttons   finding me
in the dark   the chime   the feast   our shared sleep.

Then, we are in the same room as your first wife, we are all
young again, you and she meet as if for the first time

and I'm afraid it will all happen again, just as before.
I have to interrupt it – wake up, stop you both –

HYDE PARK

– black alderwood juniper pink and
lime parakeets dart forked green streaks we
run to the pavilion hear the rain
boom and shatter the branches
conkers bounce around us like bullets
their green spikey jackets split open
a glittering ballet of rain
soaking the brick   the streets, your shirt
bayleaf and grapefruit our mouths
a laughing gutter   a river   cry me

The woman in the attic has woken up.
Her sedation has worn off. Rain is thumping

on the roof of the pavilion, she climbs on the roof.
Threatens to jump. She's banging her feet, shouting

how she *still lives in your body*, curled there
like a spiralled foetus, then bigger, a child

in a dog bed. Now she sits on the edge of your bed,
tries on your wedding veil, plays with a lighter at its hem.

The successful removal was not complete.
The buried are returning, stones release

their beautiful song after months of drought.
It's raining, it's raining hard, and the body's

jangling chains are also crows pecking
at their reflections, breaking glass,

returning day after day, shattering
all the windows in the house.

PERTAINING TO DRIFT

– to water

small boats at rest

distant on a still lake   .

I want to die in your arms

but it was like that, wasn't it –

when the rest of our lives gave up on us

and wandered away

pertaining to amniotic the twins

of birth and death   floating, linked

in their private embrace

a privacy   that brings the world   to quiet

     – a room within a room

briefly   safe

SHOES

After fifty years hard labour,
desire released my throat
and walked away.

I wanted to hurt
those who loved me, was loyal
to those that betray.

House on fire? I'll walk
into it. Broken glass? Hang on,
I'll take off my shoes.

Anxiety, a hedge on fire.
Or is it grief, still? We all

wear a little drag, doubling,
acting. But that February

you finally lost your power,
little man behind the curtain.

Oblivious. You had been in a
different dream, all along.

Our fingers hold a dim memory,
still climb into each other like vines.

Poetry, the one mistress
I will not forsake.

I push against my mind
like a heavy door and you

wobble off on your electric bike,
down the Lewisham Way.

LOVE ROOM

Blow me if we haven't gone and buried desire
and forgotten where on earth we put it.
Even the hotel's best "Love Room"
can't swim us back to erotic joy, that take-off
of a body's freedom. Is it buried in the plump
satin hearts that dangle off the door handles?
Perhaps it's in the dinky teacups? Behind
the ruched curtains or the heart-shaped
pink velvet cushions. Of course! It must be hiding
here in the trampoline-sized bed, that would be
the obvious place. But nope, nothing.

I stepped forward
expecting the usual footfall

and found thin air.
Opened a familiar cupboard

to shelves, suddenly bare.
Or, perhaps I mimed the opening

and there never was a cupboard,
there was no stair. You simply

weren't there.
Just pixels, a glimpse of smoke.

What I'd assumed solid,
overnight was broken, was dust.

I woke to a silent house, trust –
a cut line.

Though I searched for you –
snatched at spirits even when something

was clearly now nothing. Nothing
its empty shape. Silence,

don't speak to me again.

She was always in love
with someone else.
A Shakespearean comedy
but not resolved.
For someone afraid of numbers
she sure could compute
when she needed to.
Washed clean of class, of
responsibility, of love itself,
she thinks she may now be
a human stone, garlanded so
with grief and fear.

He takes her hand
and holds it against his heart.
Hands become birds,
roosting, finally at rest.
While under their feet
the gulf appears
between their desires
and the possibility
of ever achieving them.

DANCE

Another boat glides past,
its advent calendar of cabin windows,
little peepshows, dioramas of domesticity.
Art! If it's really the *Philosophy of Optimism*
– bring it on. But with so much capacity
we all have to make compromises, don't we.
Reduce life to twelve notes, temper our
human potential to be able to at least
live with ourselves. This I tell myself
as we dance on the green Mosel
and you deliver a brief lecture on why
we're alive in this best of all possible worlds.

Fields after rain. Cobbled, set with silver coin,
shining hoof prints and chevron. River that dreams

itself road. I'm foolish for lovingly kissing you,
sorrow for all the people you've hurt, a virus spreading.

The train is cancelled – a body on the track.
A man shouts at me for wearing a mask.

I'm a posh girl, so polite and forgiving,
nannying you, tripping over myself.

Why don't you fuck off and retire, sit by a river.
Watch the ducks bred to be shot by the rich,

their flights as if suiciding, their sudden hangings.
Dogs bark and bark. A branch bent across the path

like a Dubai arch. Your hands the bones
of your feet their long skeletons.

You say the purpose of life is to pass it on.
Look down into the well, a portal to the underworld

where the herd gallop, jump into where the deer live,
and the fox. Sex, I don't miss it, aside from when

I see tufts of grass growing in the mud, waving,
and when the wind is blasting in my head

and the perfume of the wood before we burn it,
like human hair. Your greedy mating above the flood line,

a statue from where my weakness stems.
I read you. The two ways of leaving, like tulips

shrivelling or mad opening. Let us be the second.

4/

SEAPLANE

I used to believe I could store beauty,
stockpile my wolfish stare and

capture it in a vault somewhere.
Insurance against the future

and its certain suffering.
On the glittered jade –

an aircrafts' tiny shadow.
Not much between us

and the four eagles that freely
display their joy, their trust

in the solidity of air
that holds them in its sway.

Below, brambles grow.
Everything surprises. Mount Tolmie,

the Garry Oaks and pale camas
– the Canadian bluebell.

The awkwardness of landscape,
I'm not afraid of it. The bent,

the clumsy, the incorrect. Faith,
I'm fifty-eight in a seaplane. Hold me.

BANFF, APRIL

Held in the mountain's open palm, the Bow
is a lifeline, an arrow.

The snow-melt of its laughter –
　　　　not trapped.

Under a thick skin of ice
　　　　the river flows

mint-green　　　glacial-cold.

Pale-furred elk
stand on a white blanket

　　　　there are cliffs and steppes of ice,
level plains to walk out on,

　　　　　　　　islands

that might maroon you.

~

The Bow struggles
        to shed its winter coat, its

stiff, creaking coat.

It levers through the valley,
insists its way –

            crooked   then straight,
then curved. Its own free country.

            ~

By the shores here in summer, yes,
they would camp and hunt,

it was a place to stay a season
then move along

            the sun-glittered highway.

Snow falls and charms the city
to Japanese woodcut, little arched bridges,
temple roof and spruce.
Seek peace and it could be here
in the alleyways of Kitsilano, the trawl
of distant traffic, the secluded
backs of houses, their wooden steps
and decks plump with snow.

A figure walks across a room
talking on a phone, another
sits at her desk, laptop opening
a sunrise on her face.
Plants and books and order,
apricot-lit windows
frame these stage sets on a life.

Distant shovels bite and scrape,
their cries half anguish, half hope.
Canada, land of safety and welcome –
though you did not always find it there,
did you, outsider? Walking in the dark,
tire tracks zippers in the snow,
unfastening off into night.

A MAN STANDS

At Trout Lake we carry hand-made lanterns;
frail fishing rods that do not kill fish.

Trembling tea-light in a red paper box,
the evening sky

indiscriminate and fragile, making up
for all we have lost. Exhaust of an idling car

darkens the air – remember, God faces two ways –
a duet for the unknown that must remain

unknown. Trees disrobe, the crowd leaves.
A man stands on a balcony. He leans forward,

silenced by the pink light, the trawl
of evening cloud threading

between the coastal mountains,
his visible/invisible wealth.

LIGHTS

– last night we rode a diamond sleigh
the lights were green and blue and a blaze

of coral fire knitted through the branches.
Blue fir trees skated across the lake

and the bear had golden eyes.
Up in the dim sky, a sickle moon hung.

A bit tired, a bit pale, she turned away
and shivered. *Nevertheless, she persisted.*

CLOUD

Crossing Canada a pulled fleece of cloud
pulled over its entirety for five hours,
aside from a glimpse of Prairie – its flat squares

a Mondrian or some other purist aiming
to reduce to abstraction. The plane's bulk
lowers itself onto England, nothing yet

but cloud beyond the small oval, then,
a sudden bloom of green – wet and bright
as if you're gazing directly into a rock pool.

SUITCASES

Gatwick at Christmas: the grey rubber
path does the rounds, a scalloped armadillo
or recycled suit of armour.

Our luggage totters by like sushi –
or humanity – tired, a little beaten,
our parcels of intention,

our pills, our clothes and shoes.
Hidden, so chosen, worried over.
The cases un-risen loaves, or

unloved children, hoping
to be picked. A rainbow belt
round that one, the hard shell of that.

BLUEBELLS

They won't be photographed, those wild girls of Kent –
show up sullen and ordinary. And you can't pick a bunch

to take home to display in the domestic interior – a spray,
a show of fragrant indigo – no, they won't play along.

Try and paint them, they'll still elude you, go mute. Mimic
themselves in chintzy parody – make of the artist yet
                                      another fool.

You have to go to them. Walk the winding paths
and breathe their sharp, damp air. Like spirits, they hover

over the earth for a few weeks. Loving the beech and oak,
all that is sunlit and dappled and green.

They sing their songs of vanquish and arrival.
Then overnight – they're gone.

THE TREES

We drink and eat in the Amber Room
stacked with books and photographs and tapestry.
Our blind neighbour suggests I write about trees –
so many species 'round here, she notes.

Sure, why not write about trees?
Their variety and histories, anything
than this circling, a lost dog after a scent,
a seedling craning for its light –

~

Start with a name:
ash, willow.

Or, the bright mane of sun
that spikes behind the oak.

Ice clings to grass all day.

A hem of polished brass
defines the beech.

Thank you weeping willow
that would hide me,

be mine
private tent.

And what of the six shadow-mountains
that paint the slope?

The cold air.
Low January light,

earth full and waiting. Thank you,
I see you, I still

see you.

~

Stone houses, cars idling and we
see each other, clear-eyed, finally.

The heart has got to open in a fundamental way.
I'm not all here. Violence against women

is completely interconnected
to violence against the land.

Don't you ever tire of knocking?
Tire of the wind chimes of your intuition,

that warn on repeat – on repeat – on repeat –
as you wander off

in the opposite direction

~

The trees listen. They stand as witness.
Speak with the land and the land

speaks to estuary, confluence, loom –
the re-troubling, the dance of the line –

folds of water, pleating, braiding.
As things rot so things grow.

Ask the water (water-walks),
wind-song that gathers itself

high in the trees. And – hear this –
listen to their reply.

DEAL

You borrowed a dish of pebbles from the beach
to bake blind – a fig tart. Good citizens, we

returned them later, poured them home.
Took a bottle. The moon rising plump and low,

making a wonderful night-drama.
We sat on the shore as if at the finest opera house,

a golden river thrown across black satin,
inviting us to get up and walk – the moon

bloomed silent, endlessly patient. Elsewhere,
plans are made to colonize, drill it for lithium.

Elsewhere crowded boats sink, sink and they also
make shore – *while ignorant armies clash by night.*

BRIDESTONES

You do nothing casual here.
Ted Hughes

High on the Pennine Moor,
an outcrop of stones – a congregation,

their elephant boulder-memory.
A woman's place, on the edge.

Here are hags, giant frozen waves,
their spy-holes and hollows.

Here are eons, brief braille of lichen
and the years of space between us.

A constellation of absence, forgiveness,
the necessary burying of hurts.

Our ageing. Words we don't and
can't say, gaps weathered into sculpture.

The fine brush-stroke
of our hard-earned lightheartedness,

(toad-rock   table-rock

           stack and loaf)

past rocks' shoulder, a blue glimpse of fields.
Mans' stone walls straight, and well meant.

We have not lived within such walls.
Our hands held in the un-farmed heather.

Millstone grit, wind-worn heads.
Hollowed cup-marks and basins.

The tiny birds that sing full-throated
on their risen thrones.

5/

There are many bridges.
We call this "The European Idea."
Yellow stars circle
a blue umbrella, rain-light
patterns the morning.

Names on graves faded
in less than a generation,
grown over by lichen, by a
new version. Many voices
silenced, spoken for, fabricated.

Silence interrogates silence.
Where they're buried is now their home,
their new Capitol.
Build the crypt first, face East.
Begin at the deathbed, with jewels,

bulbs buried like eggs at Easter.
Bulbs that grow more jewels,
that become testes, sprouting
in the warm earth, the romantic,
speaking land of rivers

that we gaze at, glazed silent
by so much we can't know –
perhaps another sphere,
perhaps even God.

~

Then we woke.
We were in a lock.

Cliffs of concrete grinding
against the boat as she
lowers herself dutifully downward.
As she works her long hours,
journeying from source to the North sea.

Aspen and silvered willow.
Island and confluence. Water
lies under the ground, but it is still there.

WATERMARK

Angels fly their gold
on battered gold within the golden city,
the slubbed fabric of its walls, its paper, its flying lions.

Flight, and a view I've lived till now to see,
to lean from a window
where the black gondolas are veiled

in widow's lace, they tug and clop
like horses stamping their breath
upon the jade. There are rubies

on the chandeliers that escort the corridor,
the benevolent channel of wooden posts
that lead us, totemic and human.

A gull angles the boat, makes a painting
of where you are. In the fog,
place of dream, of incense smoke.

Its name a bookmark for your future,
of your past. Turquoise and pink confetti
from last week's carnival gather

in little drifts between the flagstones.
The gondolas are black angels,
Viking-prowed. They have axe heads.

The Galleria an etching, a de Chirico.
Stalls of feathered masks and T-shirts,
the little dog.

~

And here's the winged Lion, the one
I might marry, for his kindness, his sun-like heart.
He hands me a mirror and I walk

slowly across the great hall, carrying it
like a tea tray, the ceiling served
dark gold, embossed like a Fabergé egg.

At La Fenice the conductor's flying arms
are also wings, and the gull
tilts against the wind.

We are propped in our carved thrones, sinking,
mended, fragile. Watermarks of silk
pattern the marble, green pools,

Rorschach ink flowering in candlelight.
The neat white shirts of the chorus
lined up like piano keys. Throw yourself

off the pinnacle of the tower,
Catastrophe. I'll give you the key
to the Kingdoms of the world.

MARYANN, REMEMBER

– that night we were twenty
and shared a double bed in Rome,
it was stiflingly hot and I wanted
desperately to caress you,
mount you like a man,
like a woman. We held back,
sleepless, rigid with desire –
at least I was. I see your mouth still
in Renaissance paintings,
the cherubs, the saints,
the Virgin in Ecstasy.

– the Lion's hot breath is a thick river flowing
into my face in the night, slain antelope liver
oozing its stench, reminder of its sacrifice.
He ate it earlier in the Italian restaurant with
ritualistic focus, as if it were a Holy Thing
placed before him, amid the ferns and Easter
lilies, the satin covers. Portraits of women,
their beautiful painted masks.

– just to float the idea: let's *not* haul the boat by oxen.
Past little Hercules, posing in his friable shrine.

When we emerge from the canal, women
are waving from the shore,

but everyone had their eyes on Corinth,
its fluid origins of democracy.

Spread your sail, oh happy heart.
In winter you can sit and think,

map the stars and rationalize your morals.
The sea today is a plaza, a busy town square

in the turquoise eye of the winds.
Everything has its logic, even the little birds

that live in the cliffs, even your short
and unaccounted-for life. Dolphin will pilot us

past pink oleander, up into the hills
where the muses watch and laugh.

Cyprus trees are our punctuation, their spires
dark and tall. Raise up your arms in prayer.

For your mother, your cattle and pacing horses.
Your broken torso. Your beautiful

and unanswered desires.

We used to say, in Rounds,
if a patient's mother died,
now she might recover.
The most chronic, entrenched.
Now she might recover.

And it would seem to happen,
the mother died and the daughter
finally clambered into her own self
like a river breaking through a dam.
The mother-boulder moved aside,

evaporating charisma and water
bursting through, gathering, dividing.
The vast gates of honey limestone
stand at the bridge from fountain to city.
Laying bare the structures

of memory and shame on which we
build our past. Second marriages
evoke incest taboos. Home, mother-
struggle, transference and safety.
Rescue me with your imaginary power.

Saxophone notes catch on the warm air.
Who would not be happy? We eat
ravioli and drink Maltese wine on a terrace.
Below shadow-figures dance
against the city wall, fireworks shatter

for Pride. This imperfect nest,
this frame. I want to love again.
Stand on that precipice. How she
flattered with her confidences, harmed
the frame with her secrets and burdens.

Seduced, as I would then seduce –
therapists, teachers, the marrieds.
I was her familiar, her intimate.
Goddess of the temples,
hand-pinched clay.

The woman's thighs, her arms.
Here is Picasso, here is Moore.
The dead ask not for reciprocity.
Who made thou, little statue,
who made thou?

SWIFTS

Hidden away, cloistered by marriage, women talk from their balconies
while the swifts circle the square, free of fantasy and ideas.

Everything is theatre. The groom's mother opens the door and
flows down the church steps in her heavy green satin. As evening nears,

furies and wraiths rise up and circle. Now she sits in a Sicilian palace,
the tall ceiling blue as any dawn, painted with cupids and temples.

Now she wants a drink. On her fingers, white chalk from the staircase walls,
a rustle of crinoline. The opera singer lifts her beautiful arms as she sings.

There are a few rooms where you can finish your life. If you have wings
you can be naked, myth an old hand at chaperoning your pornography.

Lemon trees clean our thoughts. In the morning we'll rise, breathe to prepare for a deep dive, the day a rescue and an ordeal, a battle

fought in the green reality. In the cafe, torrents of words pour from the people, a plaza of gossip and laughter. Everyone suffers, you are not the only one.

Many items are not under glass. No, Madam,
that does not mean you can touch them,

even the luscious marble with its rough glitter.
Please don't steal them, either – though that

was not said. Let's abandon the old gods –
one more victory like that and we're finished.

Lines suggest walls, walls suggest
a collection of similar things. A door suggests

the path to salvation and anything outside the wall
is extramural, where the graffito and the amuletic text

collide. The size of the material matters.
Professor, don't you mean passage?

No, that's a destroyed tomb.
He was born just two months after his death,

baptized under the green-glass panes,
amid the flames and the oil, the unwaning light.

His mother was the goddess of bloodshed and strategy,
ask her about the missing statues –

the head is missing not because it's broken,
it was never there. There are sudden summer storms,

after that, decline. We are not coming back
so let's join in the game between light and darkness.

Here comes the promise of a better afterlife –
but what we do in this life

we are certain to do in the next.
All we know, we learn from death,

the Dormant, the Sleeping Place.
Professor Parodi, quick, take me to the orchestra –

you are more extensive than magnificent,
a melancholic grandeur in the prospect.

But what is paradise? A garden, of course!
Filled with lush fruit trees and symbols of fish

whispered onto my hand.
We will know more after the excavations.

HAIKU
NORTHERN FRANCE

Flat and cloudy, a
landscape that should and should not
be painted. Light blinks

~

Tunnels are quick deaths.
Black walls acquiesce dim lamps –
moonstones vanishing

~

In an open field,
red flowers. And *the singing
will never be done*

~

Green drape of willow,
bell ringer's ropes waiting to
be pulled on. Two swans

~

Colour comes from God
and nature is a mirror
painting God in light

~

On the riverbank
a couple kiss under a
yellow parasol

EARPIECE

The woman with the tiny mouth
looks as if she'd like to flog someone
or rather, order it.

And her husband, privileged beyond belief
yet still so unhappy.
And now his earpiece won't bloody work.

He can't hear the guide telling us
how fire crawled quickly on the floor
over flowers made of tin.

About too many wars and not enough money.
How the cathedral roof was made into bullets
and where lies the saint's salted heart.

The river receives and it offers back
cloud's pattern and influence.

Trees twist from their blue-black horizons,
balloon into vast-handled amphora

that further split, throw figures, open
to become long fish, cleave again –

.brushstrokes that ink the silver
– shedding scales of light

Poplar sign the land in their single
blue brushstrokes.

Flags of iris, white
almond blossom.

The trees and fields remain as evidence,
saddening the horizons.

Threatening rain. The light failing
then shining again.

Your ascension
up pink and gold stairs.

*I can do without God
but not the power to create.*

Here is a corner of the garden, here is a church.
Not *what* but *how*.

Seventy-eight paintings in seventy-five days
till death came in a wheat field,

the wheeling sun, a host of black angels.
And here, two graves,